The HOMESCHOOL HANDBOOK

for

THE BOOK OF ESSENTIAL HOMESCHOOLING TEMPLATES

©The Life Graduate Publishing Group

No part of this book may be scanned, reproduced or distributed in any printed or electronic form without the prior permission of the author or publisher.

The HOMESCHOOL HANDBOOK
for Mom's.

SECTIONS

1. Homeschool Resource Overview	Page 5
2. Establishing 12 Month Goals	Page 7
3. Developing a Lesson Timetable	Page 11
4. Weekly Lesson Planning	Page 15
5. Weekly Tracking & Progress	Page 19
6. Establishing Important Dates	Page 23
7. Websites & Resources	Page 27
8. Major Assignment Tracking	Page 31
9. Report Cards	Page 35
10. Attendance	Page 39
11. Homeschool Supporting Resources	Page 43
12. Summary + BONUS template	Page 47

THE HOMESCHOOL HANDBOOK OF ESSENTIAL TEMPLATES

Your Free Homeschool Gift

As part of this Homeschooling Resource, we would like to provide you with a free Homeschool Timetable Template in PDF format that you can print off and use for your organization at home. This template example is provided within this resource in section 3.

To receive your **FREE GIFT**, please enter the below link in your browser.

https://thelifegraduate8265.activehosted.com/f/21

THE HOMESCHOOL HANDBOOK OF ESSENTIAL TEMPLATES

Resource Overview

Homeschooling offers students and parents the opportunity to experience a wide range of activities that may not be possible should the child attend a mainstream elementary or high school. Homeschooling can enable a stronger bond and connection with their parent that will provide a lifetime of memories and happiness.

There is a wide variety of reasons why parents may choose the homeschool pathway. This resource has been developed to provide every opportunity for the parent to structure their day, week, month, and year to achieve the best possible outcomes, both academically and through sound organizational principles.

Through a collaboration of homeschool parents, this resource has been designed as a tool that can be used across multiple areas. The homeschooling teacher can either use the template guides provided or be guided to resources that will provide all the materials they require.

Some parents may utilize this resource electronically via eBook format or choose to purchase the paperback version to assist with their planning and organization. Both options are suitable and will depend on the format that best suits your needs.

When creating the most suitable homeschooling environment, you need to do what works best for you and your child/children. Make adaptations to the templates provided in this resource if it assists to provide greater productivity.

Thank you and we hope that this resource provides the tools and information that enable your homeschooling experience to be of the highest quality for your child.

THE HOMESCHOOL HANDBOOK OF ESSENTIAL TEMPLATES

Notes

The
HOMESCHOOL
Handbook of Essential Templates
for

ESTABLISHING 12 MONTH HOMESCHOOL AND PERSONAL GOALS

THE HOMESCHOOL HANDBOOK OF ESSENTIAL TEMPLATES

Establishing Goals

The development of personal goals and those established for homeschooling is essential to provide focus and clarity on what you wish to achieve. Studies have proven that you are 30% more likely to achieve a goal if written down.

Setting firm, well-defined goals is the best way to ensure you maintain clarity in your pursuit of personal and homeschooling success. You can accomplish this by working backward from what you want to achieve. It is often referred to as 'Reverse Engineering' your goals. As an example, you couldn't get on a plane without knowing where you want to end up, and similarly, you can't make progress without knowing where you wish to go. Goals provide you with a destination you can work backward from to plot out a strategy for achieving nearly anything by breaking it down into manageable chunks. Knowing your end result allows you develop the activities and habits that are critical to achieving what you want.

The template on the next page provides a basic list of the areas to think about when establishing your goals. The best way to develop personal goals is to use a combination of the following areas and ensure you include a date that you will 'achieve' your goal by:

1. **Health**
2. **Wealth**
3. **Self & Happiness**

Feel free to use the provided template or develop your own template. When completed, reflect on it regularly, so it becomes an imprint in your subconscious mind.

Should you wish to purchase a book that further enhances your knowledge on Goal Setting, we recommend '**Magnetic Goals**' or '**The Habit Switch**' by leading Goal and Habit Formation expert, Romney Nelson

12 Month Goals

Write down the goals you wish to achieve over the next 12 months

HEALTH & FITNESS GOALS

1. ....
   ....
   Date to be achieved by   /   /

2. ....
   ....
   Date to be achieved by   /   /

SELF & HAPPINESS GOALS

1. ....
   ....
   Date to be achieved by   /   /

2. ....
   ....
   Date to be achieved by   /   /

HOMESCHOOL GOALS

1. ....
   ....
   Date to be achieved by   /   /

2. ....
   ....
   Date to be achieved by   /   /

THE HOMESCHOOL HANDBOOK OF ESSENTIAL TEMPLATES

Notes

The
HOMESCHOOL
Handbook
for

DEVELOPING YOUR HOMESCHOOL TIMETABLE

THE HOMESCHOOL HANDBOOK OF ESSENTIAL TEMPLATES

Lesson Timetable

Each homeschooling environment will be different for every family depending on your child's age, the number of homeschool children you have, your home environment, and other things like employment obligations and additional daily commitments. Therefore, it is difficult to design a 'one-size' fits all model when it comes to developing your home school timetable.

Your timetable should be developed with a structure in mind and an element of flexibility so it can be adaptive to things that come up. Most children and teenagers adapt better to structure and routine, so developing a timetable with their input will provide positive results. Having no structure or a schedule to follow can prove challenging, and this can cause a lack of focus and concentration for the homeschooled child.

When developing your school timetable or schedule, ensure you provide a balance between studies, break times every hour, and physical education sessions/games to assist with flexibility, strength, hand-eye coordination, and aerobic and anaerobic fitness. Activities like art and craft and the occasional field trip are also important to incorporate.

Each timetable should include a healthy cross-section across the academic fields to provide balance and assist with enjoyment. Areas such as writing, math, science, health, geography, music & dance, physical education, reading, and the list goes on.

The following page provides a 5-lesson p/day structure template that you could use as a guide to establish your sessions. Remember, include break/rest times in your schedule throughout the day to ensure energy levels remain at their optimum.

WEEKLY TIMETABLE
DATE COMMENCING: /   /

DAY	MONDAY	TUESDAY	WEDNESDAY	THURSDAY	FRIDAY
LESSON 1 *START TIME* : *END TIME* :	Subject	Subject	Subject	Subject	Subject
LESSON 2 *START TIME* : *END TIME* :					
LESSON 3 *START TIME* : *END TIME* :					
LESSON 4 *START TIME* : *END TIME* :					
LESSON 5 *START TIME* : *END TIME* :					

Other information to note

Weekend Information

Notes

The HOMESCHOOL Handbook for

DEVELOPMENT OF HOMESCHOOL SUBJECTS & LESSONS

THE HOMESCHOOL HANDBOOK OF ESSENTIAL TEMPLATES

Lesson Planning

The planning of your lessons will come down to the following five elements:
1. **Your time time you allocate to each class or subject in your timetable**
2. **Your desired academic outcomes**
3. **The subjects you are teaching**
4. **The age appropriateness of your lessons**
5. **The number of children you are homeschooling**

The five above elements provide the structure of your day and, therefore, your lessons over the week. As a homeschooling parent, you will have many responsibilities that are not connected to homeschooling, and consequently, the organization of your day is vital.

To assist your organization, it is encouraged to plan well ahead of time to provide a sound structure for your lessons. To do this, set aside time each week as 'Organization Time.' This may require 45 mins to 1 hour so you can have all the resources ready that you need for the week.

The timetable template provided in this resource and as a free gift will prove the initial structure but it will be the template on the following page that will give you the structure to plan and prepare each individual class or lesson ahead.

Some of your planning may require more in-depth information, while other subjects may require just a brief outline or the allocation of assignment information that you may be starting or continuing with.

Remember, the quality of your lessons will be a reflection on the quality of your planning.

DATE / /

Mom's
**HOMESCHOOL
Teacher's
Planner**

LESSON 1 SUBJECT	Lesson Information/Assignment Task
_____	Completed

LESSON 2 SUBJECT	Lesson Information/Assignment Task
_____	Completed

LESSON 3 SUBJECT	Lesson Information/Assignment Task
_____	Completed

LESSON 4 SUBJECT	Lesson Information/Assignment Task
_____	Completed

LESSON 5 SUBJECT	Lesson Information/Assignment Task
_____	Completed

DATE / /

LESSON 1 SUBJECT	Lesson Information/Assignment Task
_____	Completed

LESSON 2 SUBJECT	Lesson Information/Assignment Task
_____	Completed

LESSON 3 SUBJECT	Lesson Information/Assignment Task
_____	Completed

LESSON 4 SUBJECT	Lesson Information/Assignment Task
_____	Completed

LESSON 5 SUBJECT	Lesson Information/Assignment Task
_____	Completed

Notes

The
HOMESCHOOL
Handbook
for

TRACKING YOUR HOMESCHOOL PROGRESS

THE HOMESCHOOL HANDBOOK OF ESSENTIAL TEMPLATES

Tracking Progress

Reflecting weekly on your progress is a great way to monitor and track the goals you set out to achieve. Weekly tracking provides a sub-conscious reminder and the key actions you need to either start doing or continue to do for your homeschool classes.

Many people underestimate the importance that stopping and reflecting can have both personally and for the success of your homeschooling. As with daily gratitude journals, the pausing and reflecting allow time for you to stop, review, and then pivot if needed to continue to provide the best experience for your child or children.

Consider introducing the **STOP>REVIEW>PIVOT** & **POWER** Review Process:

STOP: Pause and consider if the information and material you are teaching is beneficial. Are the resources you are using beneficial?

REVIEW: Take note of the progress your child is making and if there are any changes you should look to implement into your homeschooling.

PIVOT: Do you need to change direction and try a new approach? Are there small changes that will make a significant difference?

POWER: Once you have completed your review and possibly made some changes, it is time to Power On with your teaching.

The Weekly Tracker template provided on the next page should be incorporated weekly and become a tool that is incorporated into your homeschool experience and resource 'tool belt.'

Progress Tracker

What are my current Top 5 Priorities I need to action?

1. _____

_____ Target Date to Complete   /   /

2. _____

_____ Target Date to Complete   /   /

3. _____

_____ Target Date to Complete   /   /

4. _____

_____ Target Date to Complete   /   /

5. _____

_____ Target Date to Complete   /   /

Other Notes or Details

Notes

The
HOMESCHOOL
Handbook
for

IMPORTANT DATES PLANNER

THE HOMESCHOOL HANDBOOK OF ESSENTIAL TEMPLATES

Important Dates

Recording important upcoming dates will help to keep a well-organized structure for your weekly homeschool experience. Having the dates recorded well in advance provides you with the opportunity to structure your weekly sessions accordingly. There will be events, activities, and appointments that come up unexpectedly, but where you can, list dates and place them either in your planner or somewhere that is easy to keep track of like your fridge door.

Please refer to the next page of a simple template that you can record your important dates or purchase a yearly planning calendar.

IMPORTANT DATES

Record the import Homeschool Year Dates

MONTH:

MONTH:

MONTH:

Notes

The
HOMESCHOOL
Handbook
for

RESOURCES AND WEBSITES

THE HOMESCHOOL HANDBOOK OF ESSENTIAL TEMPLATES

Resources & Websites

By researching the web and using various social media channels, you can locate valuable websites and resources that will be highly beneficial for your classes and planning. While you can save many websites as 'Favorites' to your browser, it is also worth your time recording them down in written format. This can also apply to the names of books or other resources that you may track down.

Other options you may consider are:
1. Joining Facebook Groups with like minded people that you can share experiences and resources with that will benefit the whole group.
2. Online bookstores that provide specific niches or topics like 'Homschooling'.
3. Review different homeschooling blogs and websites that provide key information that will assist with accumulating valuable information, books, online classes etc.

The Website and Resources Template on the next page can provide the basic structure you need, and this information can be used and easily referenced when required.

IMPORTANT WEBSITE RESOURCES

Name	Website Address

Other Books or Resources

Notes

The
HOMESCHOOL
Handbook
for

DEVELOPMENT & TRACKING OF ASSIGNMENTS

THE HOMESCHOOL HANDBOOK OF ESSENTIAL TEMPLATES

Developing Major Assignments

Recording the assignments that you set for your child forms part of an essential step as a homeschooling parent. Detailing this information will show accountability for the work you expect to be completed, what is required, and the timeframe for the assignment to be completed.

Keeping this information in an easy to find location is critical for your organization. The template on the next page has been designed to capture the following information:

1. **The date the assignment was set**
2. **The assignment/task to be completed**
3. **Notes or details**
4. **A sign off and approval signature**
5. **Grading allocated for the completed project or assignment.**

The greater the detail you can provide will enable greater clarity on what is expected of the assignment or project by your child. You may even like to consider including a progression checklist so as the child progresses through their assignment, you can mark these points off accordingly.

MAJOR ASSIGNMENTS

DATE:

Subject:	Assignment/task

Notes

Signature _____ Date _____

Grade

DATE:

Subject:	Assignment/task

Notes

Signature _____ Date _____

Grade

Notes

The
HOMESCHOOL
Handbook
for

STUDENT REPORTS

—— **THE HOMESCHOOL HANDBOOK OF ESSENTIAL TEMPLATES** ——

Report Cards

Throughout the year, you will need to assess your child's competency and their progress in each of the subject areas you have been teaching.

Completing the reports will provide an excellent tracking and ongoing review tool for you and meet the reporting requirements of a homeschool environment.

The template example developed on the next page will provide the following essential information:
1. Date
2. School Year level
3. Student Name
4. Age of Son/Daughter
5. The Reporting Period
6. Subject
7. Grading
8. Comments

Be very honest in your appraisal and provide points that will encourage your child to continue to improve. The language you use in your reporting needs to be positive and upbeat with areas they did well and areas they can improve in.

report card. _____

DATE ☐   **SCHOOL YEAR LEVEL** ☐

STUDENT NAME ☐

AGE ☐   **REPORTING PERIOD** EG. Sept – Nov ☐

SUBJECT ☐   **GRADE** ☐

COMMENTS

☐

SUBJECT ☐   **GRADE** ☐

COMMENTS

☐

SUBJECT ☐   **GRADE** ☐

COMMENTS

☐

Notes

The
HOMESCHOOL
Handbook
for

ATTENDANCE LOG

THE HOMESCHOOL HANDBOOK OF ESSENTIAL TEMPLATES

Attendance Data

Logging your child's attendance is a requirement for many states, and therefore, the daily attendance log template provided will significantly assist with this process.

The template provided has been broken up into 12 months, and therefore it is nice and easy to mark the box accordingly.

Consider using the following symbols on your attendance log:

X = Absent
/ = Half Day
F or a **'tick'** = Full Day

You may also like to have your child complete their own attendance log and play their part in the administration of homeschooling. Small tasks of responsibility for children is a great way to have them involved.

KEY
X = ABSENT
/ = HALF DAY
F = FULL DAY

ATTENDANCE LOG

MONTH

DAYS											
1											
2											
3											
4											
5											
6											
7											
8											
9											
10											
11											
12											
13											
14											
15											
16											
17											
18											
19											
20											
21											
22											
23											
24											
25											
26											
27											
28											
29											
30											
31											
TOTAL											

TOTAL DAYS PRESENT =

TOTAL DAYS ABSENT =

Notes

The
HOMESCHOOL
Handbook
for

HOMESCHOOL SUPPORTING RESOURCES

THE HOMESCHOOL HANDBOOK OF ESSENTIAL TEMPLATES

Homeschool Supporting Resources

There are many resources available that can assist your homeschooling efforts to plan and remain organized.

Two resources that The Life Graduate Publishing Group has developed specifically for the Homeschool Parent are:

1. The Homeschool Teacher's Planner
2. The Homeschool Student Planner

Both resources provide the templates to enable your homeschool experience to run smoothly.

While we encourage you to create the templates that work best for you using the guides provided in this resource, the above two resources accelerate this process by having these templates printed in bulk for a very cost-efficient price that will save you both significant time and effort.

Please refer to the next 2 pages with a summary of the books. They can be purchased via major online bookstores or by visiting www.thelifegraduate.com Bookshop and selecting the bookstore link that is most appropriate for you.

THE HOMESCHOOL TEACHER'S PLANNER 🏠

Purchase yours today via all major online bookstore or via
www.thelifegraduate.com

The Homeschool Teacher's Planner is your all-in-one, fully customizable teaching companion to help you plan, record, track and review the school year.

Designed to integrate all of the important elements of providing organization and homeschooling all into one resource, The Homeschool Teacher's Planner provides you with the structure to forward plan all of your lessons, record assignments, important yearly dates and attendance data.

Suitable for all homeschool situations and planning preferences, this homeschool planner will help you manage your home classroom with:
- Weekly lesson plans plus additional notes section
- Daily Attendance Log from the beginning of the homeschool year to the end
- Weekly Tracker to review your progress
- Important Monthly Dates to record dates, assignments and tasks
- Major Assignment templates including details, comments and the final grade
- Report Templates for each QTR to record details for each subject
- 8.5 x 11 inch Gloss Cover

Design your homeschool environment to meet your day, week and month and remain organized with planning your lessons that will play a huge role in your child's education.

The Homeschool Teacher's Planner is an ideal gift for the home-schooling parent who loves to be organised, well planned and ready to make a difference.

THE HOMESCHOOL STUDENT PLANNER

Purchase yours today via any major online bookstore or via
www.thelifegraduate.com

The Homeschool Student Progress Planner includes:
- A template for students to include their Weekly Timetable
- Weekly Planning to include all Class Lessons and Subjects
- A weekly gratitude log
- Self-Reporting Attendance Log
- Templates to Record Subject and Assignment Tasks
- Templates for the Homeschool Teacher/Parent to complete subject reports
- 8.5 x 11 inch to provide ample room to provide information
- 140 pages
- Makes an excellent companion to The Homeschool Teacher Planner resource

THE HOMESCHOOL HANDBOOK OF ESSENTIAL TEMPLATES

Summary

As mentioned in the resource overview, the purpose of The Homeschool Handbook was developed to provide several organizational templates and resources that you can use to design and implement your homeschool classes.

Homeschooling will provide a number of challenges, including how to correctly organize your environment for the best outcomes for your child or children. The templates in this resource are there to help reduce some of the problems of establishing the structure you need, and if these can help accelerate the process, then it has been a worthwhile investment of your time.

These templates will be a great start for many homeschooling parents and may also provide inspiration to create your own unique templates for future use. The best way to organize your homeschooling is by trying different templates, structures, resources and information to get the right combination that is best suited for your homeschool technique.

We hope you find the information and templates contained valuable and wish you all the very best for your homeschool journey.

Remember to grab your **Free Copy** of the PDF Timetable as shown in Section 3 as mentioned at the beginning of this book.

— THE HOMESCHOOL HANDBOOK OF ESSENTIAL TEMPLATES —

BONUS TEMPLATE
- Field Trip & Adventures -

Visiting Location

Date

Weather Conditions

Time

Names of attendees

Field Trip Details/Notes/Reflections

About
THE LIFE GRADUATE PUBLISHING GROUP

The Life Graduate Publishing Group was first established in early 2019 with the key focus on creating high-quality books and resources that will benefit customers worldwide.

Now with over 100 titles ranging from self-help books, children's books, journals, diaries, educational resources and sporting resources, The Life Graduate Publishing Group is tailoring resources specific to the needs of the customer.

The Life Graduate Publishing Group uses the world's largest Print on Demand (POD) services and therefore our books are available to anybody, anywhere in the world.

Visit. **www.thelifegraduate.com**

Notes

www.ingramcontent.com/pod-product-compliance
Lightning Source LLC
Chambersburg PA
CBHW082334060825
30747CB00010B/586